ANTAL TRAVEL G~~~~ 2024

Your Ultimate Guide To History, Cuisine, Accommodations: Navigate Like A Local And Plan Your Memorable Adventure In The Turkish Riviera.

By

LINDA N. NORMAN

Copyright page:

ANTALYA TRAVEL GUIDE 2024: Your Ultimate Guide To History, Cuisine, Accommodations: Navigate Like A Local And Plan Your Memorable Adventure In The Turkish Riviera.

Copyright © 2024 Linda N. Norman

INTRODUCTION   **5**
Overview Of The Region   7
Why Visit Antalya   9
CHAPTER 1 : PLANNING YOUR TRIP   **12**
The Best Time To Visit   12
How To Get Antalya   14
Moving Around   17
What To Pack For Your Trip   19
Entry And Visa Requirements   23
Currency And Language   26
Money-Saving Tips   28
CHAPTER 2: ICONIC SIGHTS AND NATURAL WONDERS   **32**
Kaleiçi: Ancient City Center   32
Düden Waterfalls   34
Aspendos Amphitheater   36
Konyaaltı Beach   38
Antalya Museum   40
Hadrian's Gate   42
Taurus Mountains   45
Lara Beach   47
CHAPTER 3: LODGING OPTIONS   **50**
Types of Accommodations   50
Luxurious Havens and Resorts   52
Charming Boutique Stays In Kaleiçi   54
Coastal Resorts   56
Budget-Friendly Guesthouses   59
Tips for Choosing Accommodation in Antalya   61
CHAPTER 4: LOCAL FEASTS AND CUISINE

65

Traditional Turkish Cuisine — 65

Top Restaurants in Antalya — 68

Street Food Delights — 71

Local Drink Experiences in Antalya — 74

CHAPTER 5: OUTDOOR THRILLS AND ADVENTURES — 78

Exploring The Taurus Mountains — 78

Diving in the Mediterranean — 80

Boat tours and sailing — 82

Adventure sports in the region — 85

CHAPTER 6: ART, CULTURE, AND AMUSEMENT — 89

History and Culture — 89

Antalya Museum — 91

Local Markets and Handicrafts: — 92

Folk Music and Dance Performances: — 94

Evening Entertainment Options — 95

CHAPTER 7: A WEEKLONG ITINERARY — 98

CHAPTER 8: PRACTICAL TIPS AND INFORMATION — 104

Cultural Courtesies — 104

Language And Communication Tips — 108

Basic Turkish Phrases — 110

Health And Safety Advice — 113

Emergency Contacts — 116

Communication And The Internet — 118

Essential Apps, Websites, and Maps — 120

CONCLUSION — 124

INTRODUCTION

Welcome, fellow explorer! Pause for a moment and imagine a destination that defies expectations—a city where history intertwines with modernity and nature's wonders unfold in a breathtaking spectacle. This is Antalya, a realm waiting to be discovered, and I pose a question to you: Are you ready to embark on a journey that transcends the ordinary and immerses you in the extraordinary?

Antalya, nestled along the sun-kissed Turkish Riviera, is not just a destination; it's a living narrative etched in the annals of time. As we flip through these pages together, you'll soon realize that Antalya is a city that beckons you to delve beyond the surface, inviting you to unlock its secrets and witness the fusion of ancient tales and contemporary vibrancy.

Beyond the well-trodden paths lies Kaleiçi, the beating heart of Antalya. Imagine wandering through labyrinthine streets where the echoes of centuries past reverberate against ancient walls. Hadrian's Gate stands as a sentinel, welcoming you to a realm where Roman emperors once walked. But Antalya is more than just an open-air museum; it's a living, breathing testament to the harmonious coexistence of the old and the new.

Imagine standing at the edge of Düden Waterfalls, where cascading waters paint a mesmerizing portrait of nature's grandeur. The Taurus Mountains, an unexplored canvas, invite you to traverse trails that lead to panoramic vistas and hidden enclaves. Antalya whispers tales of adventure, daring you to go beyond the postcard-perfect scenes and immerse yourself in its untold stories.

But here's the real question: Can you resist the call of the Beagle Channel, where the sea kisses the horizon, or the allure of the mythical Aspendos Amphitheater, echoing with the cheers of ancient audiences? Antalya challenges you not merely to observe but to participate—to be a storyteller in its narrative.

As we navigate the guide together, each page is an invitation to unravel Antalya's mysteries, to dance with its vibrant culture, and to savor its culinary delights. So, are you prepared to be captivated, to let

Antalya weave its magic around you? Let the anticipation build, for the journey we're about to embark upon is nothing short of a captivating odyssey. Welcome to Antalya, where every question posed is an invitation to discover the extraordinary. Let the adventure unfold!

Overview Of The Region

Antalya, a radiant jewel on the Turkish Riviera, is a destination that transcends the boundaries of the ordinary, offering a captivating blend of history, nature, and culture.

Geography:

Nestled on the southwestern coast of Turkey, Antalya beckons with a geographical panorama that weaves together the rugged majesty of the Taurus Mountains and the azure allure of the Mediterranean Sea. As you traverse the city, the Taurus Mountains stand proudly to the north, creating a dramatic backdrop that sets the stage for an unforgettable journey. Meanwhile, the coastline unveils pristine beaches, secluded coves, and a maritime wonderland waiting to be explored.

Climate:

Antalya's climate is a symphony of sunshine, with long summers and mild winters. The Mediterranean influence ensures sun-drenched days, making it an ideal destination for those seeking coastal charm and warmth. The Taurus Mountains not only contribute to the city's breathtaking vistas but also play a role in creating a microclimate that fosters lush landscapes and a diverse tapestry of flora.

Culture:
Step into the heart of Antalya, and you'll find Kaleiçi—a living testament to the city's rich cultural heritage. Enclosed by well-preserved walls, this ancient city center invites exploration through narrow cobblestone streets that whisper tales of Ottoman, Roman, and Byzantine influences. Hadrian's Gate, a Roman triumphal arch, proudly marks the passage into a world where the traditions of the past seamlessly embrace the vibrancy of the present.

Language:
While Turkish is the predominant language, fear not, for the language of hospitality is universal. English is widely understood in tourist hubs, ensuring that every visitor feels welcomed and understood. Antalya's people, known for their warmth and friendliness, invite newcomers to experience Turkish hospitality firsthand, creating an atmosphere that goes beyond mere travel—it becomes an enriching cultural exchange.

Cuisine:
Antalya's culinary scene is a sensory journey, inviting you to savor the rich flavors of Turkish

cuisine. From succulent kebabs to flavorful mezes, each dish is a celebration of tradition and taste. The local markets offer an abundance of fresh produce, and the city's restaurants serve as gateways to a gastronomic odyssey that mirrors the diverse influences that have shaped Antalya's culinary identity.

As you embark on this guide, envision Antalya not just as a destination but as a convergence of history, nature, and culture. Each element weaves together to create a tapestry of experiences, promising every traveler a sojourn that transcends the ordinary. Welcome to Antalya, where the essence of the Mediterranean unfolds in a captivating symphony of sights, tastes, and traditions.

Why Visit Antalya

Antalya, a destination that transcends the ordinary, beckons travelers with a captivating array of experiences that set it apart from the rest. Here's why you should not just visit but immerse yourself in the wonders of Antalya:

Historical Marvels:
Step into the ancient embrace of Kaleiçi, where history comes alive in the narrow cobblestone streets and well-preserved walls. Antalya boasts a rich tapestry of historical marvels, from the iconic Hadrian's Gate to the mythical Aspendos

Amphitheater. The city stands as a living testament to the civilizations that have left their mark on its landscapes.

Natural Wonders

Antalya's geography is a masterpiece of nature's artistry. From the enchanting Düden Waterfalls to the panoramic vistas of the Taurus Mountains, every corner of this city whispers the untold stories of the earth. The beaches, kissed by the Mediterranean Sea, invite relaxation, while the rugged mountains offer thrilling adventures for nature enthusiasts.

Culinary Delights:

Antalya is a gastronomic haven, inviting you to savor the flavors of Turkish cuisine in a way that is uniquely its own. From the tantalizing street-side bites to the exquisite fine dining experiences, every meal is a journey through the rich culinary heritage of the region. Fresh seafood, aromatic spices, and traditional mezes await to delight your taste buds.

Cultural Fusion:

Immerse yourself in the cultural tapestry of Antalya, where the traditions of the past seamlessly blend with the energy of the present. Whether exploring local markets filled with handicrafts, witnessing folk music and dance performances, or simply engaging with the friendly locals, Antalya offers a cultural experience that goes beyond the superficial.

Adventure Awaits:
For thrill-seekers, Antalya is a playground of adventures. Hike through the Taurus Mountains, dive into the Mediterranean's azure depths, or embark on a sailing excursion along the Beagle Channel. The city caters to outdoor enthusiasts, promising an adrenaline-pumping escapade at every turn.

Aesthetic Pleasures:
Antalya is a visual feast, from the vibrant hues of Konyaaltı Beach at sunset to the timeless beauty of ancient ruins. The city's commitment to preserving its heritage is evident in every detail, making it a paradise for photography enthusiasts. Every frame tells a story, and Antalya provides the canvas.

In essence, Antalya is not just a destination; it's an invitation to experience a harmonious blend of history, nature, and culture. The city's uniqueness lies in its ability to offer a diverse array of experiences, ensuring that every visitor discovers something extraordinary that resonates long after their journey concludes. Come to Antalya and unlock the secrets of a city that promises more than a vacation—it offers a transformative adventure.

CHAPTER 1 : PLANNING YOUR TRIP

The Best Time To Visit

Choosing the optimal time to visit Antalya is crucial to ensuring you make the most of your experience. The city experiences moderate, rainy winters and hot, dry summers due to its Mediterranean climate. Here's a breakdown of the best times to visit Antalya:

Spring (April to June):

Spring is an ideal time to visit Antalya, offering pleasant weather with temperatures ranging from 15°C to 25°C (59°F to 77°F). During this season, the landscapes burst into vibrant colors, and outdoor activities are at their peak. It's a perfect time for exploring historical sites, hiking, and enjoying the coastal charm without the intensity of summer heat.

Summer (July to August):

Summer in Antalya is characterized by hot and dry weather, with temperatures often exceeding 30°C (86°F). This is the peak tourist season, attracting sun-seekers to the beaches and outdoor enthusiasts to the Taurus Mountains. If you enjoy the lively atmosphere, water activities, and vibrant nightlife, summer is the time for you.

Autumn (September to October):

Autumn is another excellent period to visit Antalya, as the temperatures begin to cool down while still maintaining a comfortable range of 20°C to 30°C (68°F to 86°F). The summer crowds start to dissipate, making it an ideal time for a more relaxed experience. It's perfect for sightseeing, hiking, and enjoying the still-warm waters of the Mediterranean.

Winter (November to March):

While Antalya experiences a milder winter compared to other parts of Turkey, it can still be wet, especially in December and January. The range of daytime temperatures is 10°C to 15°C (50°F to 59°F). Winter is an excellent time for budget travelers, as accommodations and activities are more affordable.

It's also a unique time to explore historical sites without the crowds.

In summary, the best time to visit Antalya depends on your preferences and the type of experience you seek. Whether you prefer the lively atmosphere of summer, the blooming landscapes of spring, the tranquility of autumn, or the budget-friendly winter months, Antalya welcomes you with open arms throughout the year.

How To Get Antalya

By Air:

- **Antalya Airport (AYT):**

  The primary gateway to Antalya is Antalya Airport, situated approximately 13 kilometers (8 miles) northeast of the city center. AYT is well-connected with domestic and international flights, making it convenient for travelers worldwide. Major airlines operate regular flights, ensuring accessibility from major cities around the globe.

Transportation from Antalya Airport:

- **Taxi**:

  Taxis are readily available at Antalya Airport, providing a convenient and direct transfer to your accommodation. The journey to the city center typically takes around 20 minutes, depending on traffic conditions.

- **Shuttle Services:**

  Several shuttle services operate between the airport and various points in Antalya. These services offer a cost-effective option, and the journey time can vary based on your specific destination within the city.

- **Car Rentals:**

  Various car rental companies have counters at Antalya Airport, allowing travelers to hire a vehicle for the duration of their stay. This option is ideal for those who wish to explore the region independently.

By Land:

- **Bus Services:**

Antalya has a well-established bus network connecting it to other cities in Turkey. The main bus terminal in Antalya is the "Otogar," and intercity buses offer a comfortable and affordable mode of transportation.

- **Car:**

  For those exploring Turkey by road, Antalya is accessible via well-maintained highways. The city is well-connected to major cities like Istanbul, Ankara, and Izmir. Renting a car provides flexibility and the opportunity to explore the scenic routes leading to Antalya.

By Sea:

- **Cruise Ships:**

  Antalya's Old Harbor welcomes cruise ships, offering a unique and picturesque entry to the city. Cruise passengers can disembark and explore the historic Kaleiçi district or venture further into the city for various attractions.

Antalya's accessibility by air, land, and sea ensures that travelers have a range of options to choose from when planning their journey. Whether arriving from international destinations or exploring neighboring cities within Turkey, the transportation infrastructure ensures a seamless and enjoyable travel experience to the captivating city of Antalya.

Moving Around

Antalya offers diverse transportation options, making it convenient for visitors to explore the city and its surrounding attractions.

Public Transportation:

- **Bus:** Antalya has an efficient and affordable public bus system that connects various neighborhoods within the city and reaches suburban areas. The central bus station, "Otogar," serves as a hub for intercity and local buses.

- **Tram:** The Antalya Tramway operates along the city's coastline, providing a scenic and convenient way to travel between key points. It connects the city center with popular areas like Lara and Konyaaltı.

Private Transportation:

- **Taxi:** Taxis are readily available throughout Antalya. They provide a convenient and flexible mode of transportation, especially for short distances or when traveling with luggage. Ensure the taxi uses a meter and agree on the fare before starting the journey.

- **Car Rental:** Renting a car is a popular option for those who wish to explore Antalya and its surroundings independently. Numerous car rental agencies operate in the city, and driving allows for easy access to attractions beyond the city center.

Scenic Routes

- **Bike Rentals:** Antalya encourages eco-friendly transportation, and bike rentals are available for those wanting to explore the city at a leisurely pace. The flat terrain along the coastline makes biking an enjoyable and scenic experience.

- **Walking**: Many of Antalya's attractions are concentrated in the city center, especially in the historic Kaleiçi district. Walking allows visitors to immerse themselves in the charm of narrow streets, historic sites, and vibrant markets.

Specialized Tours:

- **Boat Tours:**Given Antalya's coastal location, boat tours are a popular way to explore the region. These tours often include visits to nearby islands, hidden coves, and opportunities for swimming in the crystal-clear Mediterranean waters.

- **Jeep Safaris:** Adventure seekers can opt for jeep safaris that take them into the Taurus Mountains, providing a thrilling off-road experience combined with panoramic views of the stunning landscapes.

Navigating Antalya is a seamless experience, with a variety of transportation options catering to different preferences and travel styles. Whether you prefer the convenience of public transport, the flexibility of a private car, or the scenic routes offered by bike rentals, Antalya ensures you can explore every corner of this captivating city.

What To Pack For Your Trip

Packing wisely is key to enjoying your Antalya experience to the fullest. The city's diverse offerings, from historical sites to stunning beaches, call for a versatile wardrobe and essential items. Here's a comprehensive list to ensure you're well-prepared for your Antalya adventure:

Clothing:

- **Light and breathable clothing**

Antalya's climate is typically warm, especially in the summer. To stay comfortable, bring clothing that is airy and lightweight.

- **Swimwear:**

  essential for enjoying Antalya's beautiful beaches and coastal activities.

- **Sun Protection:**

  sunscreen, a wide-brimmed hat, and sunglasses to shield yourself from the Mediterranean sun.

- **Comfortable Shoes:**

  Sneakers or comfortable walking shoes are recommended for exploring historical sites and navigating the city's diverse terrain.

- **Modest Attire:**

  If planning to visit religious sites, have a modest outfit, such as a shawl for women.

Practical Items:

- **Power Adapter:**

  Turkey uses Euro Plug (Type C and F) electrical outlets. Ensure you have the appropriate power adapter for your devices.

- **Travel Insurance:**

  It is always wise to have comprehensive travel insurance to cover any unforeseen circumstances.

- **Backpack or Daypack:**

  ideal for day trips, carrying essentials, and exploring without being encumbered.

- **Reusable Water Bottle:**
  ○
  Stay hydrated, especially in Antalya's warm climate.

Health and Safety:

- **Basic First Aid Kit:**

  Include essentials like band-aids, pain relievers, and any personal medications.

- **Mosquito Repellent:**

  particularly useful if you plan to explore areas near water or during the evening.

Technology and Documentation:

- **Travel Documents:**

  Passport, airline tickets, hotel reservations, and a visa (if needed).

- **Camera/Smartphone:**

  Capture the beauty of Antalya's landscapes and historical sites.

- **Portable Charger:**

  Ensure your devices stay charged, especially during day-long explorations.

Leisure and Entertainment:

- **Books/Travel Guide:**

  Enhance your understanding of Antalya's history and attractions.

- **Beach Towel:**

  perfect for a day of relaxation by the Mediterranean.

- **Snorkeling Gear:**

  Explore the underwater world if you plan on spending time in the crystal-clear waters.

Remember, Antalya offers a mix of experiences, so pack accordingly. Whether you're delving into history, enjoying the beaches, or trekking in the mountains, thoughtful packing ensures you're ready for every facet of this enchanting city.

Entry And Visa Requirements

Visa Requirements:

- **Visa Exemption:**

  Citizens of many countries, including the United States, European Union members, and several others, do not require a visa for stays of up to 90 days within a 180-day period for tourism or business purposes.

- **E-Visa:**

  For those not covered by visa exemption, Turkey offers an e-visa system. Travelers can apply online before their trip, and the process is straightforward. It's advisable to obtain the e-visa before arriving in Turkey to avoid potential delays.

- **Visa-on-Arrival:**

  Some nationalities can obtain a visa upon arrival at Turkish airports. However, it's recommended to check eligibility and the latest regulations before planning your trip.

Passport Requirements:

- **Validity:**

  Make sure the validity of your passport extends at least six months beyond the day you intend to depart Turkey.

- **Blank Pages:**

  Have at least two blank pages in your passport for entry stamps.

Arrival Procedures:

- **Customs Declaration:**

  Fill out a customs declaration form upon arrival, declaring any items subject to duty.

- **Health Declaration Form:**

  Due to health and safety measures, especially during the ongoing global situation, you might be required to fill out a health declaration form. Before you depart, confirm the most recent criteria.

Important Notes:

- **Overland Travel:**

  If arriving by land, check the visa requirements for the specific border crossing you intend to use.

- **Multiple-Entry Visa:**

  If you plan to leave and re-enter Turkey within the visa validity period, ensure you have a multiple-entry visa or the necessary arrangements to obtain a new visa.

- **Extendable Visas:**

  For those wishing to stay beyond the initial visa period, inquire about the possibility of extending your stay through local authorities.

It's crucial to stay informed about the latest visa regulations, as they may change. Check with the Turkish Embassy or Consulate in your home country for the most up-to-date information before embarking on your journey to Antalya.

Currency And Language

Currency:

- **Turkish Lira (TRY):**
  - The Turkish Lira is the official currency of Turkey. Symbol: ₺, Code: TRY. It's advisable to exchange currency upon arrival in Antalya for convenience.

- **Currency Exchange:**

  Currency exchange services are available at the airport, banks, and exchange offices throughout Antalya. It's recommended to compare rates to get the best deal.

- **Credit Cards:**

  Major credit cards (Visa, MasterCard, and, to a lesser extent, American Express) are widely accepted in hotels, restaurants, and larger shops. However, it's advisable to carry some cash, especially in more local or smaller establishments.

- **ATMs:**

  ATMs are prevalent in Antalya, allowing easy withdrawal of Turkish Lira. To prevent any problems with overseas transactions, let your bank know when you will be traveling.

Language:

- **Turkish:**

  The official language of Antalya and Turkey is Turkish. While English is widely spoken in tourist areas, it's beneficial to learn a few basic Turkish phrases to enhance your experience and show appreciation for the local culture.

- **Common Phrases:**

  Learning simple greetings like "Merhaba" (Hello), "Teşekkür ederim" (Thank you),

"Evet" (Yes), and "Hayır" (No) can go a long way in facilitating communication.

- **Translation Apps:**

  For more complex interactions, consider using translation apps to bridge language barriers. However, most locals in tourist areas are accustomed to communicating in English.

Understanding the currency and language landscape in Antalya ensures a smoother and more enjoyable experience during your stay. Whether you're navigating markets, dining in local eateries, or exploring historical sites, having a basic understanding of Turkish currency and language enriches your connection with this vibrant city.

Money-Saving Tips

Accommodation:

- **Off-Peak Travel:**

  Consider traveling during the shoulder seasons (spring and autumn) to take advantage of lower accommodation rates.

- **Local Guesthouses:**

  Opt for locally run guesthouses or boutique hotels, especially in the historic Kaleiçi district, for a more authentic experience at potentially lower costs.

Dining:

- **Street Food Exploration**

  Embrace the local street food scene for affordable and delicious options. Doner kebabs, simit (Turkish bagels), and börek (savory pastries) are popular choices.

- **Local Markets:**

  Visit local markets like the Antalya Bazaar to purchase fresh produce, snacks, and even handmade crafts at lower prices than in tourist-centric areas.

Transportation:

- **Public Transport:**

  Utilize the affordable public transportation options, including buses and trams, to explore the city and nearby attractions.

- **Walk or Bike:**

  Antalya's city center, especially Kaleiçi, is best explored on foot. Consider renting a bike for short distances, which will allow you to save on transportation costs.

Activities:

- **Free Attractions:**

  Enjoy the city's free attractions, such as the Old Harbor, Hadrian's Gate, and strolling through the charming streets of Kaleiçi.

- **Combo Tickets:**

  Some historical sites offer combo tickets, providing access to multiple attractions at a discounted rate. Check for these options when planning your visits.

Shopping:

- **Bargain at Markets:**

  Practice your bargaining skills at local markets. It's customary, and you may secure better deals on souvenirs, textiles, and spices.

- **Local Handicrafts:**

  Purchase souvenirs directly from local artisans or craft markets for unique items at reasonable prices.

General Tips:

- **Tap Water:**

  Antalya's tap water is generally safe to drink. Avoid unnecessary expenses on bottled water by carrying a reusable bottle and refilling it as needed.

- **Avoid Tourist Traps:**

  Venture away from the most touristy areas for meals and shopping to find more budget-friendly options.

By incorporating these money-saving tips, you can make the most of your Antalya experience without compromising on authenticity or enjoyment. Embrace the local culture, explore off-beaten paths, and savor the delights of this enchanting Turkish city while being mindful of your budget.

CHAPTER 2: ICONIC SIGHTS AND NATURAL WONDERS

Kaleiçi: Ancient City Center

Kaleiçi, the ancient city center of Antalya, unfolds like a living historical tapestry. Enclosed by well-preserved walls, this district is a captivating maze of narrow cobblestone streets, Ottoman-era houses, and ancient landmarks. As you wander through Kaleiçi, each step whispers the stories of civilizations that have left their mark on this enchanting city.

Hadrian's Gate:

Standing as a majestic entrance to Kaleiçi, Hadrian's Gate is a Roman triumphal arch built to honor the visit of Emperor Hadrian in the 2nd century. The intricate details of the gate, coupled with its impressive size, make it a captivating starting point for exploring the wonders within Kaleiçi.

Yivli Minare Mosque:
Dominating the skyline of Kaleiçi is the Yivli Minare Mosque, a symbol of Antalya's rich cultural heritage. The mosque, with its unique fluted minaret, dates back to the 13th century and adds an elegant touch to the city's architectural landscape.

Karatay Medrese:
Immerse yourself in the spiritual and educational history of Antalya by visiting the Karatay Medrese. This well-preserved Seljuk-era medrese, or theological school, showcases intricate tilework and architectural brilliance, offering a glimpse into the scholarly pursuits of the past.

Old Harbor:
The Old Harbor, dating back to Roman times, serves as a picturesque backdrop to Kaleiçi. Lined with charming cafes and restaurants, the harbor provides a tranquil setting for a leisurely stroll or a boat trip along the coast. The view of the old city against the backdrop of the Mediterranean is a timeless spectacle.

Clock Tower:
The Clock Tower, located in the heart of Kaleiçi, is not just a timekeeping structure but a symbol of

Antalya's endurance through the ages. Dating back to the 19th century, the tower offers panoramic views of the city and the surrounding landscapes, making it a must-visit landmark.

Kaleiçi is a testament to Antalya's ability to seamlessly blend the old and the new. As you navigate its streets, you'll find a harmonious fusion of history, culture, and modern vitality. Each corner holds a piece of Antalya's past, inviting you to step back in time and savor the charm of this ancient city center.

Düden Waterfalls

Embark on a mesmerizing journey to the Upper Düden Waterfalls, located just northeast of Antalya. Nestled amidst lush greenery, these falls cascade from a height of approximately 15 meters, creating a serene and picturesque atmosphere. The natural beauty surrounding the falls provides an ideal setting for a peaceful retreat into nature.

Lower Düden Waterfalls:
The Lower Düden Waterfalls offer a captivating spectacle as the Düden River gracefully plummets into the Mediterranean Sea. Situated near Lara Beach, these falls create a dramatic scene where the fresh river waters meet the saltwater of the Mediterranean. Visit during the golden hours to

witness the falls bathed in the warm hues of the setting sun.

Observation Points:
Several well-positioned observation points provide panoramic views of both the Upper and Lower Düden Waterfalls. Capture the beauty of the cascades against the backdrop of Antalya's coastal landscapes. These viewpoints offer ideal settings for photography enthusiasts and nature lovers alike.

Boat Tours:
For a unique perspective, consider taking a boat tour that allows you to witness the Lower Düden Waterfalls from the sea. Cruising along the coastline provides a different vantage point, showcasing the falls as they gracefully merge with the Mediterranean waters.

Park Surroundings:
The areas around the Düden Waterfalls are well-maintained parks, offering shaded pathways and picnic spots. Take a leisurely stroll along the riverbanks, breathe in the fresh air, and enjoy the soothing sound of cascading water. These parks offer a peaceful diversion from the busy metropolis.

Night Illumination:
Experience the enchantment of the Düden Waterfalls after dark when they are illuminated with

vibrant lights. The night illumination adds a magical touch to the falls, creating a romantic ambiance that transforms the natural wonder into a captivating nocturnal spectacle.

Visiting the Düden Waterfalls is not just a journey to witness the power of nature but a chance to immerse yourself in the serene beauty that defines Antalya's coastal charm. Whether admiring the falls from observation points, taking a boat tour, or enjoying a peaceful picnic in the surrounding parks, the Düden Waterfalls offer an unforgettable experience for all who venture to explore them.

Aspendos Amphitheater

The Aspendos Amphitheater, a masterpiece of ancient architecture, stands as a testament to the grandeur of the Roman era. Located approximately 25 kilometers east of Antalya, this well-preserved amphitheater is renowned for its remarkable state of conservation and the immersive experiences it offers visitors.

Architectural Marvel:
Dating back to the 2nd century AD, the Aspendos Amphitheater boasts an awe-inspiring design that has withstood the test of time. With a seating capacity of around 15,000 spectators, the amphitheater was primarily used for performances, including gladiator contests and theatrical

productions. The precision of its construction and the acoustic excellence of the theater are marvels that continue to captivate modern-day audiences.

Stage and Acoustics:
The stage of the amphitheater is remarkably well preserved, showcasing intricate details and allowing visitors to imagine the grand performances that once took place here. The exceptional acoustics of the theater amplify even the softest sounds, creating an immersive experience for those exploring the site. Clapping hands or a whispered word can be heard clearly throughout the vast space.

Annual Opera and Ballet Festival:
Aspendos Amphitheater is not merely a historical site but a venue that comes alive with cultural events. The annual Aspendos International Opera and Ballet Festival attracts artists and audiences from around the world. The ancient walls resonate with the melodies of classical performances, blending the timeless ambiance of the amphitheater with the richness of artistic expression.

Panoramic Views:
Positioned on a hill, the amphitheater offers panoramic views of the surrounding countryside and the Köprüçay River. The breathtaking landscape adds to the allure of the site, providing visitors with an opportunity to appreciate the ancient marvel against the backdrop of nature.

Visitors can walk through the corridors and stands, envisioning the gatherings of spectators in ancient times. The immersive experience allows a glimpse into the cultural and entertainment practices of the Roman period, making Aspendos Amphitheater a must-visit for history enthusiasts and those seeking a profound connection with Antalya's past.

Aspendos Amphitheater stands as a cultural treasure, inviting modern explorers to step into the ancient world of entertainment and architecture. Whether attending a performance during the festival or exploring the amphitheater's historical significance, this iconic site provides a captivating journey through time in the heart of Antalya's historical landscape.

Konyaaltı Beach

Mediterranean Tranquility:
Konyaaltı Beach, a pristine stretch along the Mediterranean coast, beckons visitors with its crystal-clear waters and panoramic views of the 8+ surrounding mountains. Located in the heart of Antalya, this urban beach offers a perfect blend of natural beauty and modern amenities, making it a popular destination for both locals and tourists.

Golden Sands and Blue Waters

The beach is renowned for its golden sands that gently meet the turquoise waters of the Mediterranean. Whether you're looking for a relaxing sunbathing session, a refreshing swim, or a leisurely stroll along the shoreline, Konyaaltı Beach provides an idyllic setting for beachgoers seeking tranquility.

Amenities and Services:

Konyaaltı Beach is well-equipped with facilities to ensure a comfortable experience for visitors. From beachfront cafes and restaurants offering delectable seafood to water sports activities such as jet-skiing and paddleboarding, the beach caters to a diverse range of interests.

Tunektepe Cable Car View:

For a breathtaking panoramic view of Konyaaltı Beach and the entire city of Antalya, take a ride on the Tunektepe Cable Car. The cable car ascends to the summit of Tunektepe Hill, providing a bird's-eye view of the coastline, mountains, and the expansive beauty of the Mediterranean Sea.

Evening Strolls and Sunset Views:

As the sun begins to set, Konyaaltı Beach transforms into a romantic haven. Evening strolls along the palm-lined promenade offer a serene atmosphere, and the beachfront becomes a popular spot to witness the mesmerizing hues of the sunset over the Mediterranean horizon.

Antalya Aquarium:
Adjacent to Konyaaltı Beach is the Antalya Aquarium, one of the largest aquarium complexes in the world. Explore the fascinating underwater world, featuring a tunnel that allows you to walk through a tank surrounded by sharks and other marine life, offering a unique and educational experience.

Konyaaltı Beach, with its natural beauty and modern amenities, invites visitors to indulge in the best of both worlds—a serene escape by the sea with the conveniences of a vibrant urban setting. Whether you're seeking relaxation under the Mediterranean sun, enjoying water activities, or marveling at the sunset, Konyaaltı Beach stands as a captivating destination along the Antalya coastline.

Antalya Museum

Treasures of Antiquity:
The Antalya Museum stands as a guardian of Turkey's rich historical legacy, housing an extraordinary collection of artifacts from various periods. Located in Konyaaltı, this museum provides a captivating journey through the ancient civilizations that once thrived in the region.

Hall of Gods and Goddesses:
One of the highlights of the museum is the Hall of Gods and Goddesses, where statues and relics from ancient cities like Perge and Aspendos are on display. Marvel at the intricacies of craftsmanship and gain insight into the religious beliefs and practices of these ancient civilizations.

Sculpture and Sarcophagus Gallery:
The Sculpture and Sarcophagus Gallery showcases an impressive array of sculptures, reliefs, and sarcophagi from different periods. The artistry displayed in these exhibits offers a glimpse into the daily life, mythology, and burial customs of the ancient inhabitants of the region.

Ancient Theater Collection:
Explore the Ancient Theater Collection, featuring artifacts related to theater and performing arts in antiquity. From masks to costumes, this section provides a unique perspective on the cultural and artistic achievements of ancient civilizations.

Museum Garden:
The Museum Garden is a tranquil space where visitors can enjoy a leisurely stroll amid ancient statues and architectural elements. The garden creates a serene atmosphere, allowing guests to connect with the artifacts in an outdoor setting.

Children's Museum:

The Antalya Museum goes beyond traditional exhibits with a dedicated children's museum. Designed to engage young minds, this interactive space introduces children to archaeology, history, and the wonders of the ancient world through hands-on activities and educational displays.

Themed Exhibitions:

The museum frequently hosts themed exhibitions that delve into specific aspects of Antalya's history and archaeology. These temporary exhibits provide fresh perspectives and highlight specific artifacts, adding depth to the overall museum experience.

The Antalya Museum serves as a captivating portal to the past, offering a comprehensive exploration of the region's cultural heritage. From grand statues to intricate artifacts, each exhibit tells a story of the civilizations that have shaped Antalya over millennia, making it a must-visit destination for history enthusiasts and those seeking a deeper understanding of Turkey's rich antiquity.

Hadrian's Gate

Gateway to Antiquity:

Hadrian's Gate, a monumental entrance to the ancient city of Antalya, stands as an iconic relic of Roman architecture and engineering. This triumphal arch, constructed in the honor of Emperor Hadrian's visit in the 2nd century AD, serves as a majestic gateway to the historical heart of Antalya.

Architectural Splendor:

The architectural splendor of Hadrian's Gate is a testament to the craftsmanship of the Roman era. The three arched gates, adorned with detailed reliefs and elegant columns, create a captivating fusion of grandeur and intricacy. As you pass through the gate, you are transported back in time, surrounded by the echoes of ancient footsteps.

Historical Significance:

Beyond its ornate aesthetics, Hadrian's Gate carries immense historical significance. The reliefs on the gate depict scenes from mythology and victories, providing a visual narrative of the Roman Empire's cultural and military prowess. The gate stands as a symbol of Antalya's resilience and cultural heritage.

City Wall Connection:

Hadrian's Gate is intricately linked to the city's fortifications, forming a part of the original city walls that once enveloped Antalya. The gate served as a passage through these formidable walls, connecting the city's past with the present and inviting visitors to explore the treasures within.

Night Illumination:

The gate takes on a magical aura during the evening when it is illuminated against the backdrop of the night sky. The warm glow accentuates the details of the reliefs and columns, offering a different perspective and emphasizing the timeless allure of this ancient entrance.

Adjacent Landmarks:
Hadrian's Gate is strategically positioned, creating a picturesque ensemble with nearby landmarks such as the Clock Tower and Hıdırlık Tower. These architectural gems, collectively known as the "trio of Antalya," enhance the overall charm of the cityscape.

Modern Meeting Point:
In addition to its historical significance, Hadrian's Gate serves as a modern meeting point within the city. Surrounded by bustling markets, lively cafes, and the vibrant energy of Antalya's city center, the gate seamlessly integrates the ancient with the contemporary.

Hadrian's Gate stands as an enduring symbol of Antalya's past and a gateway through which visitors can embark on a journey through the city's rich history. Whether admired for its architectural grandeur or appreciated as a meeting point in the heart of Antalya, this iconic monument invites all who pass through to connect with the legacy of the Roman Empire.

Taurus Mountains

Majestic Mountain Range:

The Taurus Mountains, an expansive and majestic range, form a dramatic backdrop to the Antalya region. This natural wonder extends across southern Turkey, providing a scenic and diverse landscape that captivates both nature enthusiasts and adventure seekers.

Elevated Peaks:

The Taurus Mountains boast some of Turkey's highest peaks, including Mount Tahtalı and Mount Güllük. These elevated summits offer breathtaking panoramic views of the surrounding valleys, gorges, and Mediterranean coastline. Exploring the mountainous terrain provides a refreshing escape into nature's grandeur.

Hiking Trails:

For those seeking an immersive mountain experience, the Taurus Mountains offer an extensive network of hiking trails. These trails cater to various difficulty levels, allowing hikers to choose routes that suit their preferences. As you ascend, the air becomes crisp, and the landscape unfolds in a tapestry of vibrant greenery.

Hidden Caves and Gorges:

The Taurus Mountains are dotted with hidden caves, enchanting gorges, and pristine waterfalls waiting to be discovered. Explorations into these natural wonders reveal the raw beauty of the region, with each cavern and crevice telling its own geological tale.

Nomadic Traditions:
The Taurus Mountains have been home to nomadic communities for centuries, and their traditional way of life continues to leave its mark on the landscape. Encounter shepherds guarding their flocks, and witness the enduring connection between the mountain communities and their natural surroundings.

Ski Resorts in Winter:
During the winter months, the Taurus Mountains transform into a winter wonderland. Ski resorts such as Saklıkent and Davraz offer skiing and snowboarding opportunities against the backdrop of snow-capped peaks. The contrast between the Mediterranean climate at lower altitudes and the winter landscapes higher up creates a unique and captivating experience.

Starry Nights:
Away from city lights, the Taurus Mountains provide an ideal setting for stargazing. The clear mountain skies unveil a celestial panorama, offering a chance to marvel at the constellations and the Milky Way in all their splendor.

The Taurus Mountains, with their rugged beauty and diverse ecosystems, invite exploration and provide a respite from the coastal allure of Antalya. Whether hiking along scenic trails, discovering hidden caves, or experiencing the magic of winter sports, the Taurus Mountains stand as a natural wonder that enriches the overall tapestry of Antalya's landscape.

Lara Beach

Golden Sands and Azure Waters:
Lara Beach, situated on the eastern side of Antalya, is a coastal gem that captivates visitors with its golden sands and crystal-clear azure waters. Stretching along the Mediterranean coastline, the beach offers a picturesque setting for those seeking sun, sea, and relaxation.

Long Sandy Stretch:
One of the defining features of Lara Beach is its expansive and pristine sandy stretch. The beach provides ample space for sunbathing, leisurely strolls along the shore, and various water activities. Whether you prefer to bask in the sun or take a refreshing dip in the Mediterranean, Lara Beach offers a serene escape.

Luxury Resorts and Entertainment:
Lara Beach is renowned for its upscale resorts that line the coastline. These establishments not only provide luxurious accommodations but also offer a

range of amenities, including beachfront bars, restaurants, and entertainment options. Visitors can indulge in a pampering stay while enjoying the stunning views of the Mediterranean.

Dining by the Coast:
The beach is dotted with seaside restaurants where visitors can savor delicious Turkish and international cuisine with the soothing sound of waves in the background. Dining at Lara Beach offers a delightful blend of culinary experiences and coastal ambiance, making it the perfect setting for a romantic dinner or a casual meal by the water.

Water Sports and Activities:
For those seeking a bit more adventure, Lara Beach provides opportunities for various water sports and activities. From jet skiing to parasailing, the beach caters to thrill-seekers looking to add an adrenaline rush to their coastal retreat.

Sunset Serenity:
As the day draws to a close, Lara Beach transforms into a scene of unparalleled beauty during sunset. The sun dips below the horizon, casting warm hues across the sky and sea. This serene moment creates a tranquil atmosphere, ideal for an evening stroll or a romantic sunset-viewing experience.

Lara Beach, with its combination of natural beauty, luxurious accommodations, and seaside charm, stands as a testament to the allure of Antalya's Mediterranean coastline. Whether you seek relaxation, adventure, or a bit of both, Lara Beach invites you to indulge in the coastal oasis it gracefully presents to every visitor.

CHAPTER 3: LODGING OPTIONS

Types of Accommodations

- **Luxurious Havens and Resorts:**

  Antalya boasts a selection of upscale resorts and five-star hotels, each offering a lavish escape. Positioned along the pristine coastline, these luxurious havens provide guests with world-class amenities, including private beaches, spa facilities, and gourmet dining experiences. The opulent comfort combined with panoramic views of the Mediterranean Sea creates an indulgent retreat.

- **Boutique hotels in Kaleiçi:**

  Kaleiçi, the historic district of Antalya, is home to charming boutique hotels that weave together modern comfort and historical charm. These smaller establishments feature unique architecture and personalized service, providing guests with an intimate and culturally immersive experience. Staying in a boutique hotel in Kaleiçi allows visitors to be surrounded by the ambiance of the ancient city center.

- **All-Inclusive Beachfront Hotels:**

  Antalya offers numerous all-inclusive beachfront hotels, providing guests with comprehensive packages that include accommodations, meals, and various recreational activities. These hotels, often situated along the city's stunning beaches, are ideal for travelers seeking a hassle-free vacation experience where all needs are catered to within the confines of the resort.

- **Pensions and Guesthouses:**

  For budget-conscious travelers looking to immerse themselves in local charm, Antalya offers a variety of pensions and guesthouses. Especially prominent in Kaleiçi, these accommodations provide a more intimate experience. Run by friendly hosts, these establishments offer insights into the city's culture and the opportunity to discover hidden gems within the historic district.

- **Hostels and Backpacker Accommodations:**

Antalya caters to the backpacker community with budget-friendly hostels and shared accommodations. These options foster a social atmosphere, making them ideal for solo travelers or those seeking to connect with fellow adventurers. Beyond affordability, hostels often provide communal spaces and activities, enhancing the overall experience for budget-conscious travelers.

Luxurious Havens and Resorts

- **Maxx Royal Belek Golf Resort:**

Situated in Belek, this resort is synonymous with luxury, featuring elegant architecture, private villas, and a championship golf course. Guests indulge in spa treatments, gourmet dining, and exclusive beach access, making it a haven for those seeking opulence.

- **Regnum Carya Golf & Spa Resort:**

  This resort combines modern sophistication with natural beauty. Guests enjoy private beaches, a stunning golf course, and a spa offering a range of wellness experiences. The resort's architecture seamlessly integrates with its lush surroundings. It is located in Kadriye Bölgesi.

- **Mardan Palace:**

  Boasting a palatial setting in Lara, Mardan Palace is an architectural marvel located at Kundu Mah. It features lavish interiors, expansive pools, and an exclusive beach. With an emphasis on personalized service, it offers a regal experience for those seeking the pinnacle of luxury.

- **Voyage Belek Golf & Spa:**

  Located in Belek, this resort caters to discerning travelers with its combination of modern design and natural landscapes. Guests enjoy a private stretch of beach, numerous pools, and a world-class spa. The resort's commitment to excellence is evident in its attention to detail.

- **Rixos Premium Belek:**

  Situated on the shores of the Mediterranean, Rixos Premium Belek is a haven for luxury enthusiasts. The resort features private villas, multiple swimming pools, and a wealth of dining options. Guests can unwind in the spa or engage in watersports along the pristine coastline.

These luxurious havens and resorts in Antalya redefine the concept of upscale hospitality, offering a spectrum of experiences that range from regal opulence to serene sophistication. Each establishment presents a unique blend of architectural brilliance, personalized service, and breathtaking natural surroundings, making them sought-after destinations for those seeking the epitome of luxury in this coastal paradise.

Charming Boutique Stays In Kaleiçi

- **Tuvana Hotel:**

  The Tuvana Hotel, nestled in the heart of Kaleiçi, exudes historic charm with its Ottoman-era architecture. The boutique hotel features individually decorated rooms, a courtyard with citrus trees, and a rooftop terrace offering panoramic views. Guests experience personalized service in an intimate and authentic setting.

- **Deja Vu Boutique Hotel:**

  This quaint hotel captures the essence of Kaleiçi with its stone walls and wooden accents. Deja Vu Boutique Hotel offers cozy rooms adorned with antique furnishings. The courtyard provides a peaceful retreat, and the hotel's central location allows guests to explore the cobbled streets and historical landmarks on foot.

- **Puding Marina Residence:**

  Overlooking the marina, Puding Marina Residence blends modern comfort with historical elements. The boutique stay features tastefully decorated rooms, each with its own character. The courtyard pool, surrounded by lush greenery, offers a tranquil escape within this vibrant district.

- **Alp Pasa Hotel:**

  With its stone walls and wooden details, the Alp Pasa Hotel transports guests to a bygone era. The boutique stay features rooms with unique layouts and a garden courtyard. The hotel's commitment to preserving historical elements while providing modern conveniences enhances the overall charm of the stay.

- **White Garden Pansion:**

  The White Garden Pansion offers an intimate and cozy retreat in Kaleiçi. The boutique accommodation features whitewashed walls and a lush garden. Guests can enjoy a homemade Turkish breakfast in the courtyard, immersing themselves in the tranquility of this charming palace.

These charming boutique stays in Kaleiçi offer a blend of historical ambiance, personalized service, and a unique sense of place. Each establishment allows guests to immerse themselves in the enchanting atmosphere of Antalya's old town while enjoying modern comforts.

Coastal Resorts

- **Cornelia Diamond Golf Resort & Spa:**

  Situated on the shores of the Mediterranean, Cornelia Diamond Golf Resort & Spa in Belek offers a luxurious coastal retreat. The resort boasts direct beach access, multiple pools, and a championship golf course. Guests can indulge in spa treatments while enjoying panoramic views of the sea.

- **Rixos Sungate:**

  Nestled between the Taurus Mountains and the Mediterranean Sea, Rixos Sungate in Beldibi offers a coastal haven with a private beach. The resort features a vast pool complex, water sports facilities, and an array of dining options. The coastal setting provides a serene backdrop for a relaxing getaway.

- **Crystal Prestige Elite Hotel:**

  Overlooking the Mediterranean in Lara, Amara Prestige stands as a coastal oasis. With its expansive beachfront, multiple swimming pools, and a pier extending into the sea, guests can immerse themselves in the beauty of the coastline. The resort's architecture maximizes views of the sea from various vantage points.

- **Susesi Luxury Resort:**

  Susesi Luxury Resort, located in Belek, offers a coastal escape with a focus on elegance and comfort. The architecture of the resort blends in perfectly with the natural surroundings. Guests can enjoy beachfront activities, relax by the pools, and savor gourmet cuisine with sea views.

- **Delphin Imperial Hotel Lara:**

  Boasting a prime location on Lara Beach, the Delphin Imperial Hotel Lara provides an all-inclusive coastal experience. The resort features a private sandy beach, water parks, and a variety of entertainment options. Guests can enjoy the sea breeze while lounging in the beach cabanas.

These coastal resorts in Antalya provide a harmonious blend of luxurious accommodations, seaside relaxation, and a wealth of amenities. Whether seeking a tranquil escape or an active beach holiday, these resorts offer diverse experiences against the backdrop of the mesmerizing Mediterranean coastline.

Budget-Friendly Guesthouses

- **Blue Sea Garden:**

  Located in the heart of Kaleiçi, the Blue Sea Garden offers budget-friendly accommodations with a touch of Turkish hospitality. The guesthouse features simple yet comfortable rooms and a cozy courtyard. Its central location allows guests to explore the historic district without straining their budget.

- **Secret Palace Pansion:**

  Nestled among the narrow streets of Kaleiçi, Secret Palace Pansion provides affordable rooms with a charming ambiance. The guesthouse captures the essence of the old town and offers a tranquil escape. Guests can enjoy a budget-friendly stay while being in close proximity to local attractions.

- **Dedekonak Pension:**

  Dedekonak Pension, a family-run guesthouse in Kaleiçi, provides a warm and welcoming atmosphere for budget-conscious travelers. The pension offers clean and cozy rooms, and guests can relax in the garden courtyard. The affordability of the Dedekonak Pension makes it a popular choice for those exploring Kaleiçi on a budget.

- **Efsali Hotel:**

  The Efsali Hotel offers budget-friendly accommodations in Kaleiçi, emphasizing simplicity and affordability. The guesthouse provides basic yet comfortable rooms, allowing guests to allocate their budget for exploring the vibrant surroundings. Its central location ensures convenient access to Kaleiçi's attractions.

- **Hadrianus Hotel:**

  The Hadrianus Hotel, situated within the historic walls of Kaleiçi, caters to budget travelers seeking a convenient base for exploration. The guesthouse offers modest rooms with essential amenities. The affordability of the Hadrianus Hotel allows guests to allocate more resources to experiencing the local culture and attractions.

These budget-friendly guesthouses in Kaleiçi cater to travelers seeking affordable yet comfortable accommodations within the charming ambiance of Antalya's historic old town. The simplicity of these guesthouses allows visitors to allocate their resources to exploring the rich cultural heritage and vibrant streets of Kaleiçi.

Tips for Choosing Accommodation in Antalya

When selecting accommodation in Antalya, consider these essential tips to ensure a comfortable and enjoyable stay tailored to your preferences:

- **Proximity to Attractions:**

  Choose accommodations that align with your planned activities. Whether you prefer the historic charm of Kaleiçi, beachfront relaxation, or proximity to specific attractions, selecting a location that suits your interests will enhance your overall experience.

- **Reviews and Ratings:**

  Utilize online reviews and ratings on reputable travel platforms. Previous guests often shared insights into the quality of service, cleanliness, and overall satisfaction. Consider recent reviews to ensure the information is current and reflective of the accommodation's current standards.

- **Amenities and Services:**

  Evaluate the amenities and services offered by different lodging options. Whether you prioritize a pool, spa services, free Wi-Fi, or proximity to public transportation, choosing accommodation that aligns with your preferences ensures a more tailored and enjoyable experience.

- **Accommodation Type:**

  Consider the type of accommodation that suits your travel style. Whether it's a luxury resort, a boutique hotel, a budget-friendly guesthouse, or a cozy pension, each type offers a unique experience. Match your choice to your preferences and budget for a more satisfying stay.

- **Budget Considerations:**

  Set a realistic budget for accommodation and explore options within that range. Antalya offers a diverse range of lodging, allowing you to find a comfortable stay without exceeding your budget. Look for special offers or package deals that may enhance the overall value.

- **Location Safety:**

  Prioritize safety by researching the safety of the chosen neighborhood or area. While Antalya is generally considered safe for tourists, understanding the local surroundings can contribute to a more secure and relaxed stay.

- **Cancellation Policies:**

  Check the accommodation's cancellation policies before booking. Understanding the terms and conditions can be crucial, especially if your travel plans are subject to change. Flexible cancellation policies offer peace of mind in uncertain situations.

- **Accessibility:**

  Consider the accessibility of the accommodations. If you plan to explore different parts of Antalya, proximity to public transportation or major roads may be essential. Alternatively, if you seek a secluded retreat, accessibility to local attractions may be less of a concern.

- **Local Culture and Authenticity:**

  For a more immersive experience, choose accommodation that reflects the local culture. Boutique hotels in Kaleiçi or traditional guesthouses can provide a more authentic experience, allowing you to connect with the rich history and ambiance of Antalya.

- **Booking Platforms:**

  Utilize reputable booking platforms to secure your accommodation. Websites and apps often offer a range of choices, and many provide reviews, photos, and detailed information to assist in your decision-making process.

By considering these tips, you can navigate the array of accommodation options in Antalya and select the one that aligns with your preferences, ensuring a memorable and enjoyable stay in this vibrant Turkish destination.

CHAPTER 4: LOCAL FEASTS AND CUISINE

Traditional Turkish Cuisine

Antalya, with its rich cultural heritage, offers a gastronomic adventure steeped in the flavors of traditional Turkish cuisine. This chapter explores the essence of Turkish culinary traditions, showcasing iconic dishes that have stood the test of time.

- **Kebabs and Grills:**

  Turkish cuisine is renowned for its mastery of kebabs and grills. From the succulent Adana kebab to the flavorful shish kebab, these grilled delights are often accompanied by fragrant rice, grilled vegetables, and traditional flatbreads, creating a symphony of tastes.

- **Mezes and appetizers:**

  The Turkish dining experience often begins with an array of mezes, small appetizers that tantalize the taste buds. These may include hummus, muhammara, dolma, and cacık. Mezes are designed for sharing and set the stage for the main course.

- **Turkish Breakfast (Kahvaltı):**

  A traditional Turkish breakfast is a leisurely affair, featuring an assortment of cheeses, olives, tomatoes, cucumbers, jams, honey, and various types of bread. This hearty breakfast is accompanied by çay (Turkish tea) or Turkish coffee, creating a delightful start to the day.

- **Koftes and meatballs:**

  Turkish koftes, seasoned ground meat formed into small patties or balls, are a staple of Turkish cuisine. Served with rice or in sandwiches, these savory delights come in various regional styles, each with its own unique blend of spices.

- **Baklava and Turkish Sweets:**

  No exploration of Turkish cuisine is complete without indulging in the delectable world of Turkish sweets. Baklava, a layered pastry filled with nuts and honey, takes center stage. Other treats include Turkish delight (lokum) and künefe, offering a symphony of sweetness.

- **Pide and Lahmacun:**

  Pide, often referred to as Turkish pizza, features a boat-shaped flatbread topped with various ingredients, including meat, cheese, and vegetables. Lahmacun, a thin, round flatbread topped with minced meat and herbs, is a popular street food delicacy.

- **Turkish Tea and Coffee:**

  Turkish tea (çay) holds a special place in Turkish culture and is served in small tulip-shaped glasses. Turkish coffee, prepared with finely ground coffee beans, is a rich and aromatic beverage often enjoyed after meals.

- **Dining Customs and Etiquette:**

  Turkish dining customs emphasize communal sharing. Meals are often enjoyed with family and friends, fostering a sense of togetherness. It is customary to express gratitude by saying "Afiyet olsun" (may it be good for your health) after a meal.

Exploring traditional Turkish cuisine in Antalya is a journey through time, savoring dishes that reflect the culinary heritage of the region. From the vibrant colors of mezes to the rich aromas of grilled kebabs, each bite is an invitation to experience the cultural richness of Turkish gastronomy.

Top Restaurants in Antalya

- **Seraser Fine Dining:**

  Seraser Fine Dining stands as a culinary gem in Antalya, offering an exquisite dining experience that harmonizes traditional Turkish flavors with contemporary flair. Located in the heart of the city, this restaurant captures the essence of Turkish hospitality through its culinary artistry.

  Culinary Highlights: Signature dishes, a curated wine selection, and a blend of traditional and modern Turkish flavors.

  Ambiance: sophisticated and warm, with a tastefully decorated interior and the option for al fresco dining.

- **Vanilla Lounge:**
  - ○

    Vanilla Lounge is a chic establishment that fuses Turkish and international influences to create a diverse and sophisticated menu. Known for its creative culinary presentations and elegant setting, the restaurant caters to those seeking a modern twist on Turkish gastronomy.

    Culinary Highlights: Fusion dishes, creative presentations, and an extensive menu.

    Ambiance: stylish and contemporary, with modern decor and a vibrant atmosphere.

- **Pio Gastro Bar & Bistro:**
  - ○

    Pio Gastro Bar & Bistro is a culinary hotspot in Antalya, blending Mediterranean and Turkish flavors with a modern twist. The restaurant's innovative approach to cuisine, coupled with a stylish setting, makes it a go-to destination for those seeking a gastronomic adventure.

    Culinary Highlights: Innovative dishes, Mediterranean-Turkish fusion, and a diverse menu.

Ambiance: trendy and modern, with a lively atmosphere and a focus on culinary creativity.

- **Aynali Restaurant:**

Aynali Restaurant is celebrated for its panoramic views of the Mediterranean Sea and the Antalya coastline. The restaurant combines a stunning location with a menu that highlights both Turkish and international cuisines. Guests can enjoy a dining experience that seamlessly blends culinary excellence with breathtaking vistas.

Culinary Highlights: seafood specialties, Turkish classics, and a diverse menu.

Ambiance: elegant and scenic, with a focus on providing a memorable dining experience.

- **Hayal Kahvesi Restaurant:**

Hayal Kahvesi Restaurant is a charming eatery located in the heart of Antalya's old town, Kaleiçi. Known for its cozy atmosphere and emphasis on Turkish comfort food, the restaurant offers a delightful escape into the traditional flavors of the region. It is a perfect spot for those seeking an authentic taste of Turkish cuisine in a quaint setting.

Culinary Highlights: Comforting Turkish dishes, mezes, and traditional desserts.

Ambiance: rustic and welcoming, with a focus on providing a homely dining experience within the historic ambiance of Kaleiçi.

These top restaurants in Antalya offer a diverse range of culinary experiences, from traditional Turkish delights to innovative fusion cuisine. Each establishment reflects the vibrant and dynamic food scene in Antalya, inviting guests to embark on a gastronomic journey through the rich flavors of the region.

Street Food Delights

- **Midye Dolma Stalls**:

  Antalya's streets come alive with the enticing aroma of midye dolma, a popular street food featuring mussels stuffed with seasoned rice. Numerous stalls dot the coastal areas, offering a quick and flavorful snack for those exploring the city's vibrant streets.

Culinary Highlights: Fresh mussels, seasoned rice, and a squeeze of lemon create a delectable combination.

- **Simit Carts:**

Simit, a circular bread crusted with sesame seeds, is a staple of Turkish street food. Simit carts can be found throughout Antalya, providing locals and visitors with a convenient and satisfying snack. Pair it with cheese or olives for an authentic taste.

Culinary Highlights: Crispy exterior, soft interior, and the perfect balance of sesame flavor.

- **Kumpir Kiosks:**

Kumpir, a Turkish-style baked potato, takes street food to a whole new level. Kumpir kiosks in Antalya allow customers to customize their loaded potatoes with a variety of toppings, including cheese, vegetables, and meats, creating a hearty and indulgent experience.

Culinary Highlights: baked potato base, a myriad of toppings, and a satisfying combination of flavors.

- **Döner Kebab Stands:**

  Döner kebabs are a ubiquitous street food in Antalya, and the city boasts numerous stands serving this savory delight. Marinated meat, often lamb or chicken, is cooked on a vertical rotisserie and served on a flatbread with fresh vegetables and flavorful sauces.

  Culinary Highlights: tender, marinated meat, freshly baked flatbread, and a variety of condiments.

- **Tantuni Vendors:**

  Tantuni is a popular street food originating from Mersin, and its presence in Antalya adds to the city's diverse culinary scene. Tantuni vendors offer thin strips of seasoned meat wrapped in flatbread, creating a savory and satisfying handheld meal.

  Culinary Highlights: spiced meat, fresh vegetables, and a flavorful flatbread wrap.

- **Gözleme Stalls:**

  Gözleme, a traditional Turkish flatbread filled with various ingredients such as cheese, spinach, and minced meat, is skillfully prepared at gözleme stalls found in Antalya. The aroma of freshly cooked gözleme wafts through the air, inviting passersby to indulge in this delightful treat.

  Culinary Highlights: thin flatbread, flavorful fillings, and the option for a personalized touch.

Antalya's street food scene offers a delightful array of flavors, providing locals and visitors with quick and tasty options to enjoy while exploring the city's charming streets and vibrant neighborhoods. Each street food delight adds a unique touch to the culinary tapestry of Antalya.

Local Drink Experiences in Antalya

- **Turkish Tea (Çay):**

  Turkish tea, or çay, is an integral part of Turkish culture and a ubiquitous beverage in Antalya. Served in small, tulip-shaped glasses, çay is a symbol of hospitality. Whether enjoyed in traditional tea houses or at street-side cafes, the ritual of sipping Turkish tea provides a soothing experience.

- **Turkish Coffee:**

  Turkish coffee is a rich and aromatic beverage with a distinctive preparation method. Finely ground coffee beans are simmered with water and sugar in a special pot called a cezve. The result is a strong and flavorful coffee that is often enjoyed slowly, accompanied by Turkish delight.

- **Ayran:**

  Ayran is a traditional Turkish yogurt drink that serves as a refreshing counterpart to the rich flavors of Turkish cuisine. Made with yogurt, water, and a pinch of salt, ayran is a cooling beverage often enjoyed with kebabs and grilled meats, providing a perfect balance to savory dishes.

- **Rakı:**

  Rakı, often referred to as the national spirit of Turkey, is an anise-flavored alcoholic drink. It is typically consumed with water and ice, turning cloudy when mixed. Rakı holds cultural significance and is often enjoyed during social gatherings, accompanied by mezes and lively conversations.

- **Şalgam Suyu:**

Algam suyu is a unique fermented beverage made from black carrot juice, turnips, and salt. It has a slightly tangy and salty taste, making it a distinctive local drink. Algam suyu is often paired with street food, providing a flavorful and traditional beverage option.

- **Boza:**

Boza is a traditional Turkish fermented wheat beverage with a slightly sweet and tart flavor. It is often enjoyed during the winter months and is known for its unique consistency. Topped with roasted chickpeas or cinnamon, boza offers a cozy and nostalgic drink experience.

- **Meyan Şerbeti:**

Meyan şerbeti, or licorice sherbet, is a sweet and herbal beverage made from licorice root. It is known for its soothing properties and is often consumed as a refreshing drink. Meyan şerbeti is a delightful choice for those looking to experience a taste of traditional Turkish herbal beverages.

- **Salep:**

  Salep is a warm and comforting drink made from the powdered tubers of a type of orchid. It is often associated with winter and is flavored with cinnamon. Salep has a thick and creamy consistency, making it a cozy choice for chilly evenings.

Exploring the local drink experiences in Antalya provides a glimpse into the rich tapestry of Turkish beverages, each contributing to the city's culinary charm and cultural heritage.

CHAPTER 5: OUTDOOR THRILLS AND ADVENTURES

Exploring The Taurus Mountains

Hiking Horizons:

The Taurus Mountains stand as a haven for hiking enthusiasts, offering an extensive network of trails that wind through pristine landscapes. Whether you're an avid trekker or a casual hiker, the Taurus Mountains cater to all skill levels. Trail options vary from leisurely walks showcasing panoramic views to challenging routes that lead to hidden gems tucked away in the mountainous terrain.

Trekking Adventures:

For those seeking a more immersive experience, trekking in the Taurus Mountains unveils the raw beauty of the region. Multi-day treks provide the opportunity to traverse diverse ecosystems, from lush forests to high-altitude plateaus. The adventurous can explore ancient pathways that connect mountain villages, immersing themselves in the cultural tapestry of the Taurus Mountains.

Birdwatching Bliss:

The Taurus Mountains serve as a sanctuary for birdwatchers, boasting a rich avian population. From elusive raptors soaring high above to colorful songbirds nestled in the trees, the mountains provide a captivating spectacle for bird enthusiasts.

Various vantage points offer ideal spots to observe and identify the diverse bird life inhabiting this natural haven.

Photography Hotspots:
Photography enthusiasts are in for a treat amidst the Taurus Mountains' picturesque landscapes. Every turn in the trail reveals postcard-perfect scenes, from cascading waterfalls and alpine meadows to rugged cliffs that catch the golden hues of sunrise and sunset. The mountains serve as a living canvas for capturing the beauty of nature in all its splendor.

Thrill-seekers can elevate their Taurus Mountains experience by engaging in a variety of adventure sports. Rock climbing enthusiasts can scale the rugged cliffs, while paragliders can take to the skies for a bird's-eye view of the mountainous panorama. The Taurus Mountains cater to the adrenaline-fueled adventurer, offering an array of activities to spice up the exploration.

Exploring the Taurus Mountains transcends mere physical activity; it's an immersive journey into the heart of a natural wonderland. Whether you're chasing mountain peaks, reveling in the diversity of flora and fauna, or capturing the essence of the landscape through your lens, the Taurus Mountains invite you to embrace the thrill of discovery and connect with the untamed beauty that defines this majestic mountain range.

Diving in the Mediterranean

Underwater Paradise:
Embark on a mesmerizing journey beneath the surface as we delve into the enchanting world of diving in the Mediterranean. Antalya, with its crystal-clear waters and vibrant marine life, beckons divers to explore an underwater paradise that captivates the senses.

Diverse Dive Sites:
Antalya boasts an array of dive sites, each offering a unique glimpse into the Mediterranean's rich underwater tapestry. From ancient shipwrecks to vibrant coral reefs, divers can choose from a diverse range of locations that cater to both novice and experienced divers.

Caverns and Caves:
Dive into the mysterious allure of underwater caverns and caves that punctuate the Mediterranean seabed. These hidden gems provide an otherworldly experience as sunlight filters through underwater tunnels, illuminating the hidden chambers and marine life within.

Marine life encounters:
The Mediterranean's azure depths are home to a kaleidoscope of marine life. Dive alongside schools of colorful fish, encounter majestic sea turtles, and witness the graceful movements of rays. The

underwater world in this part of the Mediterranean is a living spectacle waiting to be explored.

Historical Wrecks:
Antalya's waters hold echoes of the past with the presence of historical wrecks submerged beneath the surface. Divers can uncover the secrets of ancient maritime history as they navigate around well-preserved shipwrecks, each telling a silent tale of bygone eras.

Clear Visibility:
The Mediterranean's renowned clear visibility enhances the diving experience, allowing divers to marvel at the intricate details of underwater landscapes. With visibility often exceeding 30 meters, divers can witness the full spectrum of marine life and geological formations that make each dive a visual feast.

Dive Centers and Facilities:
Antalya boasts a plethora of dive centers equipped to cater to divers of all levels. Whether you're a beginner eager to take your first plunge or an experienced diver seeking new challenges, the region's dive centers offer professional guidance and a seamless diving experience.

While diving in the Mediterranean is possible year-round, each season unveils unique highlights. Spring and summer bring warm waters and increased marine activity, while autumn offers quieter dives and the chance to witness different species. Winter provides the opportunity for more experienced divers to explore the depths in solitude.

Dive responsibly and contribute to the preservation of the Mediterranean's marine ecosystems. Antalya emphasizes conservation efforts, and divers are encouraged to adhere to sustainable practices, ensuring the underwater world remains an untouched paradise for generations to come.

Diving in the Mediterranean off the shores of Antalya is an invitation to explore a realm of wonders beneath the waves. Whether you're drawn to historical mysteries, vibrant marine life, or the tranquility of underwater caves, the Mediterranean's embrace is bound to leave an indelible mark on every diving enthusiast.

Boat tours and sailing

Nautical Adventures Await:
Set sail on an unforgettable maritime journey as we explore the allure of boat tours and sailing in the Mediterranean waters off Antalya. The region's pristine coastline, hidden coves, and azure seas create the perfect canvas for nautical adventures that promise relaxation, exploration, and a touch of luxury.

Diverse Boat Tours:

Antalya offers a myriad of boat tours catering to various preferences. From leisurely cruises along the coast to exhilarating speedboat adventures, visitors can choose from a diverse range of boat tours. Whether you seek a family-friendly excursion, a romantic sunset cruise, or a thrilling exploration of secluded bays, Antalya has the perfect boat tour for every occasion.

Sailing Amidst History:

Discover the historical richness of the Mediterranean coast while sailing on traditional wooden gulets or modern sailboats. These vessels provide an intimate and authentic sailing experience, allowing you to navigate the same waters once traversed by ancient mariners. Explore historical sites, including sunken cities and ancient harbors, as you sail along this storied coastline.

Island Hopping Adventures:

Antalya's proximity to picturesque islands sets the stage for captivating island-hopping adventures. Join boat tours that weave between islands, each with its own unique charm and allure. Whether it's the tranquil atmosphere of Kekova Island, the vibrant energy of Rabbit Island, or the historical significance of Simena, island-hopping unveils a mosaic of experiences.

Snorkeling and Swimming Stops:
Most boat tours include opportunities for snorkeling and swimming stops in secluded coves and bays. Dive into the crystal-clear Mediterranean waters to explore vibrant underwater ecosystems, encounter marine life, and bask in the refreshing embrace of the sea. These stops add an element of aquatic exploration to your sailing adventure.

Sunset Cruises:
Elevate your sailing experience with a sunset cruise along the Antalya coastline. Whether aboard a private yacht or a shared boat tour, witnessing the sun dip below the horizon, casting hues of orange and pink across the sky, creates a magical and romantic atmosphere. Sunset cruises are a perfect way to unwind and savor the beauty of the Mediterranean.

Luxury Yachting Experiences:
Indulge in the epitome of luxury with private yacht charters that provide a personalized and opulent sailing experience. Cruise along the coast in style, enjoying first-class amenities, gourmet dining, and the privacy of your exclusive floating retreat. Luxury yachting in Antalya offers a lavish escape on the tranquil waters of the Mediterranean.

Sailing Schools and Courses:
For those eager to try their hand at sailing, Antalya hosts sailing schools and courses catering to all skill levels. Learn the art of navigation, master the sails, and embrace the freedom of sailing under the expert guidance of seasoned instructors. Sailing courses provide both education and adventure on the open sea.

Ecotourism and Marine Conservation:
Antalya emphasizes ecotourism and marine conservation efforts. Participate in boat tours that promote responsible practices, including wildlife observation without disturbance and waste reduction measures. Supporting sustainable boat tours contributes to the preservation of the region's marine ecosystems.

Embark on a maritime odyssey as boat tours and sailing in Antalya invite you to explore the Mediterranean's treasures. Whether you seek relaxation under the sun, aquatic adventures, or the romance of a sunset cruise, the open waters off Antalya offer an array of experiences that celebrate the beauty of the sea.

Adventure sports in the region

Brace yourself for an adrenaline-infused exploration as we dive into the world of adventure sports in the Antalya region. With its diverse landscapes, from rugged mountains to azure waters, Antalya sets the stage for an array of heart-pounding activities that cater to the daring and the adventurous.

Rock-Climbing Escapades:

Antalya's rocky landscapes beckon rock climbing enthusiasts to ascend vertical cliffs and rugged formations. The region offers a variety of climbing routes, from beginner-friendly to challenging ascents that test the skills of even the most seasoned climbers. The juxtaposition of stunning views and the thrill of conquering heights makes rock climbing in Antalya an unparalleled adventure.

Paragliding Soars to New Heights:

Take to the skies with paragliding adventures that offer a bird's-eye view of Antalya's breathtaking scenery. Launch from elevated points such as Mount Tahtali or Babadag and soar over coastal landscapes, ancient ruins, and azure waters. The sensation of gliding through the air provides an exhilarating experience for thrill-seekers.

Off-Roading in the Taurus Mountains:

Unleash your adventurous spirit with off-roading excursions into the rugged Taurus Mountains. Hop aboard a 4x4 vehicle and traverse off-the-beaten-path routes, conquering challenging terrains and exploring hidden gems that are inaccessible by conventional means. Off-roading adventures offer a thrilling blend of exploration and adrenaline.

Canyoning through Nature's Playground:

Delve into the heart of nature with canyoning adventures that take you through the region's stunning gorges. Abseil down waterfalls, navigate through narrow canyons, and leap into crystal-clear pools. Canyoning in Antalya is a sensory-rich experience that combines the excitement of exploration with the natural beauty of the landscape.

Quad Biking Across Varied Landscapes:

Quad biking enthusiasts can rev up their engines and embark on thrilling rides across Antalya's varied landscapes. From dusty trails through pine forests to sandy paths along the coast, quad biking adventures provide an exciting way to explore the region's diverse terrain while satisfying the need for speed.

Scuba Diving in Underwater Realms:

Antalya's coastal waters invite scuba diving enthusiasts to plunge into vibrant underwater realms. Explore underwater caves, discover ancient artifacts, and encounter a diverse array of marine life. With clear visibility and a rich underwater ecosystem, scuba diving in Antalya offers a captivating glimpse into the mysteries of the Mediterranean.

Balloon Safaris over Cappadocia:

For a unique adventure, consider a hot-air balloon safari over the surreal landscapes of Cappadocia, just a short distance from Antalya. Soar above fairy-tale-like rock formations and valleys, witnessing the sunrise painting the sky in hues of pink and gold. Balloon safaris provide a serene yet awe-inspiring adventure.

Antalya's diverse terrain transforms the region into an adventurer's playground. Whether scaling cliffs, gliding through the air, or conquering rapids, the array of adventure sports available in Antalya caters to those who seek the perfect blend of excitement and natural beauty.

CHAPTER 6: ART, CULTURE, AND AMUSEMENT

History and Culture

Rich Tapestry of Antalya's Past:
Antalya's cultural landscape is a vibrant tapestry woven with threads of history dating back thousands of years. As a city with roots in ancient civilizations, Antalya stands as a testament to the passage of time and the convergence of diverse cultures.

Ancient Heritage Sites:
Explore the remnants of Antalya's ancient past through well-preserved archaeological sites. The city boasts structures from various periods, including the Hellenistic, Roman, and Byzantine eras. Marvel at the intricate details of Hadrian's Gate, a triumphal arch built to honor the Roman Emperor Hadrian, and witness the grandeur of the Antalya Museum, home to artifacts spanning centuries.

Roman Influence:
Antalya served as an important Roman port city, known as Attaleia, during the Roman period. The influence of Roman architecture is evident in structures like Hadrian's Gate and the Roman Harbor, showcasing the city's significance in the ancient Roman world.

Byzantine Legacy:
The Byzantine era left an indelible mark on Antalya, with structures like the Yivli Minaret, a stunning example of Seljuk architecture that dates back to the 13th century. The Kesik Minaret, originally a Byzantine church converted into a mosque, is another testament to the city's layered history.

Seljuk Architecture:
The Seljuk Turks, who held sway over Antalya in the 12th and 13th centuries, contributed to the city's architectural richness. The Yivli Minaret, adorned with geometric patterns and Arabic inscriptions, exemplifies Seljuk architecture and stands as an iconic symbol of Antalya.

Ottoman Heritage:
Antalya's journey through history continued with the Ottoman Empire. The city features Ottoman architecture, seen in structures like the Murat Pasha Mosque and the Clock Tower. These landmarks provide glimpses into the Ottoman influence that shaped Antalya during this period.

Antalya's history and culture intertwined seamlessly, creating a city where ancient echoes resonate alongside contemporary expressions. Explore the layers of time in archaeological sites, appreciate the diversity of architectural styles, and immerse yourself in the living culture that defines this captivating Mediterranean destination.

Antalya Museum

Antalya Museum, a modern architectural gem, unfolds a narrative of time through its extensive collection of archaeological treasures. The museum's design provides a contemporary backdrop to artifacts spanning millennia, offering a seamless journey from prehistoric epochs to the Byzantine period.

Prehistoric Origins and Classical Marvels:

Begin your exploration in the prehistoric galleries, where the Paleolithic and Neolithic artifacts showcase the earliest human endeavors in the region. Journey through the Hellenistic and Roman eras, marveling at sculptures, reliefs, and everyday objects that encapsulate the influence of ancient Greece and Rome on Antalya's cultural tapestry.

Byzantine Legacy and Ottoman Transition:

The museum gracefully transitions to the Byzantine period, revealing intricate icons and artifacts that speak to the city's religious and artistic heritage. Explore the Seljuk and Ottoman exhibits, witnessing the cultural shift that marked a transformative chapter in Antalya's history. Admire the craftsmanship of ceramics, manuscripts, and architectural elements that bear witness to centuries of influence.

Sculptures as Timeless Narratives:
Antalya Museum's impressive sculpture collection serves as a visual chronicle of artistic expression. From divine depictions to frozen portraits, each sculpture tells a story of craftsmanship and cultural significance. Interactive displays complement the exhibits, providing context and depth to the historical narratives woven into the stone and bronze masterpieces.

Preservation and Cultural Stewardship:
Beyond being a repository of antiquities, the Antalya Museum stands as a guardian of cultural heritage. Regular special exhibitions add dynamic layers to the museum experience, ensuring that every visit offers fresh insights into Antalya's rich history. Through preservation efforts and educational initiatives, the museum invites visitors to connect with the roots that define the city's identity, fostering a profound sense of cultural continuity.

Local Markets and Handicrafts:

Old Bazaar in Kaleiçi:
Dive into the heart of Antalya's vibrant culture by exploring the Old Bazaar in Kaleiçi. This bustling market, steeped in history, weaves through narrow cobblestone streets, offering a sensory-rich experience. Stroll past traditional Ottoman houses as the aroma of spices and the colors of handwoven

textiles beckon you to discover a treasure trove of local crafts.

Traditional Handicrafts:
Antalya's markets showcase an array of traditional handicrafts, each telling a story of skilled artisanship passed down through generations. From intricately designed carpets and kilims to hand-painted ceramics, these crafts reflect the rich cultural heritage of the region. Engage with local artisans, watch them at work, and bring home a piece of Antalya's artistic legacy.

Flavors of the Bazaar:
The Old Bazaar is not only a haven for crafts but also a culinary adventure. Sample local delights like Turkish delight, dried fruits, and aromatic spices. Let the flavors of the bazaar tantalize your taste buds as you explore stalls brimming with olives, cheeses, and other culinary delights unique to the region.

Contemporary Expressions:
While rooted in tradition, Antalya's markets also embrace contemporary expressions of art and craftsmanship. Discover modern interpretations of traditional items, from chic fashion pieces to contemporary art installations. The juxtaposition of old and new within the market stalls creates a dynamic and eclectic atmosphere that mirrors Antalya's evolving cultural landscape.

Folk Music and Dance Performances:

Rhythmic Beats of Tradition:
Immerse yourself in the lively beats and melodies of traditional Turkish folk music that reverberate through Antalya. Folk music in the region is a rhythmic celebration of cultural heritage, with each tune carrying the essence of centuries-old traditions. Listen to the soulful sounds of instruments like the bağlama and zurna, transporting you to a world where music becomes a vibrant storyteller.

Expressive Dance Traditions:
The dance performances in Antalya are a visual feast, expressing the vivacity of Turkish culture. Traditional dances, such as the lively Halay and the energetic Horon, showcase the rich tapestry of regional dance traditions. Dancers adorned in colorful costumes move with grace and precision, creating a mesmerizing spectacle that captivates audiences and reflects the spirit of communal celebration.

Cultural Festivals and Events:
Antalya's cultural calendar comes alive with festivals and events that feature dynamic folk music and dance performances. Attendees can witness skilled performers bring age-old traditions to life on outdoor stages or within historic venues. Whether it's the intoxicating rhythm of the Kafkas Dance or

the elegant steps of the Zeybek, these performances provide a profound connection to the cultural heartbeat of Antalya.

Interactive Cultural Experiences:
For those eager to engage with the cultural heritage on a deeper level, Antalya offers interactive experiences where visitors can join in traditional dances and learn the steps themselves. These participatory events create a sense of community and foster an appreciation for the skill and artistry involved in preserving and sharing these ageless traditions.

Antalya's folk music and dance performances are more than mere spectacles—they are living expressions of a rich cultural heritage. Whether enjoyed as a vibrant backdrop to a festival or experienced firsthand in interactive settings, these performances invite you to become a part of the rhythmic and expressive symphony that defines the cultural soul of Antalya.

Evening Entertainment Options

Open-Air Concerts at the Aspendos Amphitheater:

As the sun sets over Antalya, the historic Aspendos Amphitheater transforms into a captivating venue for open-air concerts. Nestled amidst ancient ruins, this well-preserved amphitheater echoes with the melodies of live performances, ranging from classical music to contemporary tunes. Witness the magic of music under the starlit sky, surrounded by the aura of antiquity.

Cultural Performances at Local Venues:

Antalya's evenings come alive with cultural performances at various local venues. From traditional music ensembles to modern dance troupes, these performances showcase the city's artistic diversity. Attend a live show at one of the theaters or cultural centers, immersing yourself in the vibrant expressions of Antalya's performing arts scene.

Nighttime Strolls in Kaleiçi

Kaleiçi, Antalya's charming old town, offers a different kind of evening entertainment. Take a leisurely stroll through its narrow cobblestone streets, where the warm glow of lanterns and the sounds of live music from quaint cafes create a romantic ambiance. Enjoy a drink at a rooftop bar, offering panoramic views of the city as it twinkles in the night.

Dinner Cruise Along the Coastline:

Experience a blend of entertainment and gastronomy with a dinner cruise along Antalya's coastline. Sail under the moonlit sky, enjoying a delectable Turkish dinner accompanied by live music and dance performances. The gentle sea breeze, the shimmering reflections on the water, and the rhythmic beats of the onboard entertainment make for an enchanting evening on the Mediterranean.

Antalya's evening entertainment options cater to diverse tastes, offering a mix of historical ambiance, cultural richness, and contemporary delights. Whether you prefer the classical resonance of the amphitheater, the cultural vibes of local performances, the romantic ambiance of old town strolls, or the maritime magic of a dinner cruise, Antalya ensures your nights are filled with unforgettable experiences.

CHAPTER 7: A WEEKLONG ITINERARY

Day 1: Arrival and Acclimation in Antalya

Morning: Arrival and Check-In

Arrive in Antalya and settle into your chosen accommodation.

Take a relaxing morning to acclimate to the city's ambiance.

Afternoon: Explore Kaleiçi

Begin your journey in the heart of Antalya, in Kaleiçi.

Stroll through the charming, narrow streets, discovering historical sites like Hadrian's Gate and Hıdırlık Tower.

Have a leisurely meal at a nearby eatery.

Evening: Sunset Boat Tour

Experience the enchanting Mediterranean coastline with a sunset boat tour.

Sail along the tranquil waters, witnessing the sun dip below the horizon.

Enjoy dinner on board, surrounded by the mesmerizing hues of the sunset.

Day 2: Ancient Echoes at Perge and Aspendos

Morning: Explore Perge

Venture to the ancient city of Perge, known for its well-preserved ruins.

Discover the grandeur of the Roman theater, agora, and stadium.

Afternoon: Aspendos Amphitheater

Visit the iconic Aspendos Amphitheater, renowned for its architectural brilliance.

Explore the ancient aqueduct and the surrounding historical complex.

Evening: Dinner at a Local Gem

Conclude the day with a delightful dinner at one of Kaleiçi's hidden gems.

Experience the local culinary scene in the historical heart of Antalya.

Day 3: Leisure in Kaleiçi and Sunset Dinner Cruise

Morning: Leisure in Kaleiçi

Spend the morning leisurely exploring Kaleiçi's local markets and charming alleys.

Discover hidden cafes and boutiques showcasing local handicrafts.

Afternoon: Relaxation and Preparation

Enjoy a leisurely afternoon, perhaps indulging in a traditional Turkish bath.

Prepare for an enchanting evening ahead.

Evening: Sunset Dinner Cruise

Experience a romantic sunset dinner cruise along the coastline.

Enjoy a delectable dinner with live music as the sun sets over the Mediterranean.

Day 4: Natural Wonders at Düden Waterfalls and Lara Beach

Morning: Düden Waterfalls

Visit Düden Waterfalls, where the waters cascade into the Mediterranean.

Enjoy a peaceful morning, surrounded by nature.

Afternoon: Lara Beach Relaxation

Head to Lara Beach for a relaxing afternoon.

Unwind on the sandy shores or take a dip in the Mediterranean.

Evening: Dinner with a Coastal View

Enjoy dinner with a view at one of Lara Beach's seaside restaurants.

Soak in the coastal ambiance as you dine by the Mediterranean.

Day 5: Exploration in Side and Leisure at Konyaaltı Beach

Morning: Ancient Side

Travel to the ancient city of Side.

Explore the well-preserved ruins, including the Temple of Apollo and the ancient amphitheater.

Afternoon: Leisure at Konyaaltı Beach

Head to Konyaaltı Beach for a relaxing afternoon.

Explore the beach promenade, indulge in beachside activities, and enjoy a seaside lunch.

Evening: Dinner in Kaleiçi

Return to Kaleiçi for a delightful dinner at one of its charming restaurants.

Experience the vibrant nightlife in the historic quarter.

Day 6: Antalya Museum and Cultural Experience

Morning: Antalya Museum

Spend the morning delving into the rich historyat the at the Antalya Museum.

Explore the diverse exhibits, from prehistoric artifacts to Ottoman treasures.

Afternoon: Kaleiçi Markets

Wander through the vibrant markets in Kaleiçi.

Indulge in local flavors and shop for traditional handicrafts.

Evening: Cultural Performance

Attend a traditional Turkish folk music and dance performance in the evening.

Immerse yourself in the rhythmic beats and expressive dance traditions.

Day 7: Leisure and Farewell

Morning: Leisure in Antalya

Enjoy a leisurely morning exploring Antalya at your own pace.

Revisit favorite spots or discover hidden gems.

Afternoon: Farewell Lunch

Conclude your weeklong journey with a farewell lunch at a local restaurant.

Reflect on the memories created during your Antalya adventure.

This refined weeklong itinerary ensures a perfect blend of ancient wonders, natural beauty, cultural experiences, and moments of relaxation, all complemented by the unforgettable experience of a sunset boat tour along the Mediterranean.

CHAPTER 8: PRACTICAL TIPS AND INFORMATION

As you embark on your Antalya adventure, arming yourself with practical tips and essential information ensures a seamless and enjoyable journey through this Mediterranean marvel. Here's a comprehensive guide to enhance your experience.

Cultural Courtesies

Antalya, with its rich tapestry of culture, welcomes visitors with warmth and hospitality. Embrace these cultural courtesies to enhance your experience in this Mediterranean jewel:

- **Greetings:**

    Merhaba: The Turkish word for "hello," accompanied by a smile, is a friendly and respectful greeting.

    Teşekkür ederim: Express your gratitude with "Thank you."

- **Modest Attire:**

  Respect for Religious Sites: When visiting mosques or religious sites, dress modestly. Out of respect, it's traditional to cover your knees and shoulders.

- **Shoes Off Indoors:**

  Home and Certain Establishments: In many homes and specific establishments, it is customary to remove your shoes upon entering. Take note of cues and emulate them.

  ### Respect for Elders:

- Greeting Elders: When entering a room, it's customary to greet the eldest or most senior person first. A polite nod or a slight bow is a sign of respect.

- **Hospitality and Tea Culture:**

  Turkish Tea Ritual: Tea holds a special place in Turkish culture. Accepting a cup of tea is a gesture of hospitality. It's polite to accept, even if you only take a sip.

- **Guest of Honor:** If invited to someone's home, you may be treated as the guest of honor. Express your gratitude for their hospitality.

- **Use of the Right Hand:**

Handshakes and Gestures: In Turkish culture, the right hand is considered cleaner and more appropriate for greetings and gestures. When offering or receiving something, using the right hand is polite.

- **Dining Etiquette:**

Waiting for the Host: Wait for the host or the oldest person to start the meal before you begin eating. It's a sign of respect.

Leaving a Little on the Plate: Leaving a small amount of food on your plate signifies that you are full and satisfied.

Understanding Turkish Politeness:

- **Politeness is valued**: Turks place a high value on politeness. Using phrases like "Lütfen" (please) and "Teşekkür ederim" (thank you) is appreciated.

- **Respecting Personal Space:** While Turks are warm and friendly, respecting personal space is important. Avoid standing too close to others.

Cultural Awareness in Religious Spaces:

- **Silence in Mosques:** When visiting mosques, maintain a quiet and respectful demeanor. It is traditional to take off your shoes before going inside.

- **Dress Modestly:** Cover your shoulders and knees when entering religious sites. Women may be required to cover their hair.

Environmental Respect:

- **Preserving Nature:** Antalya boasts stunning natural landscapes. Be a responsible tourist by being mindful of the environment and not littering.

Cultural courtesies in Antalya extend beyond mere gestures; they embody a genuine connection to the region's history and traditions. By embracing these customs, you not only show respect but also enrich your travel experience in this captivating destination

Language And Communication Tips

When navigating the vibrant cultural tapestry of Antalya, effective communication goes beyond language barriers. Here are essential tips to enhance your interaction with locals:

Politeness and Respect:

- **Formality Matters:** Turks often appreciate formality in communication. Using "Siz" (formal) instead of "Sen" (informal) is a courteous approach, especially with new acquaintances.

- **Courtesy Phrases:** Incorporate common courtesy phrases like "Lütfen" (please) and "Teşekkür ederim" (thank you) into your conversations.

Non-Verbal Communication:

- **Body Language:** Pay attention to non-verbal cues. A nod signifies understanding, and a warm smile transcends language barriers.

- **Hand Gestures**: Be mindful of hand gestures, as interpretations can vary. Simple, universally understood gestures are often the safest choice.

English in Tourist Areas:

- **Widespread Understanding:** English is commonly spoken in tourist-centric areas. However, learning a few basic Turkish phrases showcases cultural respect.

- **Local Phrases:** While English is prevalent, locals appreciate the effort to learn basic local phrases, fostering a deeper connection.

Addressing Locals:

- **Polite Titles:** Use polite titles like "Bey" (Mr.) or "Hanım" (Mrs.) when addressing individuals. It adds a touch of courtesy to your conversation.

- **Respectful Tone:** Adopt a respectful and friendly tone. Turks value communication that is both courteous and approachable.

Listening Actively:

- **Engage in Conversations:** Actively engage in conversations to show interest in the local culture. Listen attentively, fostering a genuine connection.

- **Seek Clarification:** If uncertain about something, don't hesitate to seek clarification. Locals appreciate your eagerness to understand.

Embracing a Local Accent:

- **Practice Pronunciation:** Embrace the local accent by practicing common phrases. Locals appreciate the effort, even if your pronunciation isn't perfect.

- **Ask for Guidance:** If unsure about pronunciation or meaning, don't hesitate to ask for guidance. Locals are often happy to assist.

Effective communication in Antalya is a blend of verbal and non-verbal cues, coupled with a genuine respect for local customs. By incorporating these tips, you not only facilitate smoother interactions but also enrich your overall experience in this captivating Mediterranean destination.

Basic Turkish Phrases

In the heart of Antalya, a few Turkish phrases can open doors to deeper cultural connections. Here are some essential phrases to make your journey even more enriching:

Greetings:

Merhaba: Hello

Günaydın: Good morning.

İyi günler: Good day

İyi akşamlar: Good evening

Hoşça kal: Goodbye (when someone is leaving).

Güle güle: Goodbye (in response to someone leaving)

Politeness and Gratitude:

Lütfen: Please

Teşekkür ederim: Thank you

Rica ederim: You're welcome

Özür dilerim: I'm sorry.

Affedersiniz: Excuse me/pardon

Basic Communication:

Evet: Yes

Hayır: No

Nasılsınız?: How are you? (formal)

Nasılsın?: How are you? (informal)

Ben iyiyim, teşekkür ederim: Thank you; I'm OK.

Directions and Common Phrases:

Evet, doğru: Yes, correct.

Nereye?: Where?

Sağ: Right

Sol: Left

Tuvalet nerede?: Where is the restroom?

Numbers:

Bir: One

İki: Two

Üç: Three

Dört: Four

Beş: Five

Embracing local culture:

Sizden bir şey sorabilir miyim? May I ask you something? (formal)

Hangi yöne gidiyorsunuz? Which way are you going? (formal)

Beni anlıyor musunuz? Do you understand me? (formal)

Embrace these phrases, and you'll find that locals in Antalya warmly respond to your effort to connect with their language and culture.

Health And Safety Advice

Ensuring your well-being is paramount as you embark on your Antalya adventure. This is a guide to safety and health:

Hydration in the Mediterranean Climate:

- **Stay Hydrated:** Antalya can have warm temperatures, especially during the summer. Carry a reusable water bottle and stay hydrated, especially if engaging in outdoor activities.

- **Avoid Dehydration:** Enjoy local beverages, but balance them with water, especially in the sun-drenched coastal areas.

Sun Protection:

- **Sunscreen:** The Mediterranean sun can be intense. Apply sunscreen with a high SPF, wear a hat, and use sunglasses to protect yourself from UV rays.

- **Timing Matters**: Plan outdoor activities during the cooler parts of the day to minimize sun exposure.

Medical Facilities and Health Precautions:

- **Know Medical Facilities**: Familiarize yourself with nearby medical facilities. Your accommodation or local guide can provide this information.

- **Emergency Services:** Dial 112 for emergency medical assistance.

- **Insurance**: Make sure your travel insurance is comprehensive and includes emergency medical coverage.

- **Prescriptions:** If you have any prescribed medications, bring an ample supply and a copy of your prescription.

Safety in Outdoor Activities:

- **Adventure Sports Caution:** If participating in adventure sports, follow safety guidelines provided by professionals. Check the credentials of activity providers.

- **Hiking and Trekking:** If exploring nature trails, inform someone about your plans, carry essentials, and be aware of your surroundings.

Mosquito Protection:

- **Mosquito Repellent**: In certain seasons, especially in more rural areas, mosquitoes can be prevalent. Use mosquito repellent and consider wearing long sleeves and pants during the evening.

Antalya's breathtaking landscapes and vibrant culture await, and by prioritizing your health and safety, you can fully savor the wonders of this Mediterranean gem.

Emergency Contacts

Ensuring your safety and well-being is a top priority during your time in Antalya. Here are some essential emergency contacts to keep in mind:

Emergency Services:

Dial 112: This all-encompassing emergency number connects you to medical, fire, and police assistance. It's the go-to number for immediate help in any emergency situation.

Police:

Dial 155: For non-emergencies or situations that require police assistance but are not urgent, dial the police hotline.

Tourist Police:

Tourist Police Hotline: Dedicated to assisting tourists, the Tourist Police can be reached through their hotline. If you encounter any issues or need tourist-specific assistance, don't hesitate to call.

Medical Emergencies:

Hospital/Emergency Medical Services: Be aware of the location of the nearest hospital or emergency medical services. Dial 112 for medical emergencies.

Consulate/Embassy:

Contact Information: If you are a foreign visitor, know the contact details of your country's consulate or embassy in Antalya.

Fire:

Dial 118: In case of a fire emergency, dial 118 to connect with the fire department.

Coastal Safety:

Coast Guard (Sahil Güvenlik): If you are near the coast and encounter a maritime emergency, contact the Coast Guard.

Roadside Assistance:

Roadside Assistance (Otoyol Yardım): If you experience vehicle trouble on major highways, roadside assistance is available. Know the contact details for assistance.

Antalya prioritizes the safety of its residents and visitors. Save these emergency contacts in your phone and hope for a safe and enjoyable stay in this captivating Mediterranean destination.

Communication And The Internet

Staying connected in Antalya is key to enhancing your travel experience. Here's a guide to communication and internet access:

SIM Cards:

- **Purchase a Local SIM Card:** Upon arrival, consider getting a local SIM card. This provides you with a local phone number and cost-effective data plans.

- **Major Carriers:** Look for SIM cards from leading Turkish carriers like Turkcell, Vodafone, or Türk Telekom.

Wi-Fi Availability:

- **Accommodations:** Most hotels, hostels, and guesthouses in Antalya offer complimentary Wi-Fi for guests. Confirm this when checking in.

- **Public Spaces:** Cafes, restaurants, and public spaces commonly provide free Wi-Fi. Look for signage indicating its availability.

- **Internet Cafes:**

Option for Longer Sessions: If you need an extended internet session, you can find internet cafes in the city offering computer access and high-speed internet.

Essential Apps:

- **Translation Apps**: Download language translation apps like Google Translate to bridge language gaps.

- **Navigation Apps:** Utilize navigation apps like Google Maps for seamless exploration.

Connectivity in Tourist Areas:

- **Tourist Hotspots:** Popular tourist areas in Antalya are well-equipped with connectivity. You'll find Wi-Fi hotspots and excellent mobile network coverage.

Internet Etiquette:

- **Public Spaces**: Be mindful of internet usage etiquette in public spaces. Avoid loud video calls and use headphones for multimedia content.

Emergency Connectivity:

- **Offline Maps**: Download offline maps to navigate without a constant internet connection, especially in more remote areas.

- **Emergency Numbers:** Save emergency contact numbers offline in case you need them without internet access.

Staying connected ensures you can easily navigate Antalya's wonders, communicate with locals, and share your experiences with friends and family back home. Whether you're posting photos of historic sites or staying in touch with loved ones, Antalya offers ample connectivity options.

Essential Apps, Websites, and Maps

Equipping yourself with the right digital tools enhances your Antalya journey. Here are essential apps, websites, and maps to facilitate a seamless exploration:

Navigation Apps:

Google Maps: is a reliable navigation app offering detailed maps, real-time traffic updates, and local business information. Download offline maps for areas with limited connectivity.

- **Maps.me:** is an offline mapping app that allows you to navigate without an internet connection. Download Antalya maps in advance for easy exploration.

Language and Translation Apps:

- **Google Translate:** is a powerful tool for translating text and speech. Download the offline language pack for Turkish to assist in communication.

- **DuoLingo**: Learn basic Turkish phrases with this interactive language learning app.

Local Information Websites:

GoTurkey, the official tourism website of Turkey, provides comprehensive information on attractions, events, and travel tips.

Antalya City Guide: ExploreAntalya.net offers a city guide with detailed information on attractions, dining, and activities.

Transportation Apps:

- **Uber/Taxi Services**: Uber is available in some areas of Antalya. Alternatively, local taxi services and ride-sharing apps can be convenient for transportation.

- **Moovit**: For public transportation information, Moovit helps you navigate Antalya's bus and tram systems.

Currency Converter:

- **XE Currency:** Stay updated on currency exchange rates with this reliable currency converter app.

Weather Apps:

- **AccuWeather**: Check the local weather forecast to plan your activities accordingly.

Safety Apps:

SOS Turkey: The official emergency app for Turkey provides quick access to emergency numbers and services.

- **Smart Traveler**: If you're a U.S. citizen, the Smart Traveler app by the U.S. Department of State offers travel alerts and information.

Social Media:

- **Instagram/Facebook**: Share your Antalya experiences with friends and family. Follow local accounts for insights into events and activities.

Remember to download essential apps and maps before your trip, especially those offering offline functionality. These tools will enhance your Antalya adventure, providing information and assistance at your fingertips.

CONCLUSION

As we draw the final curtain on this Antalya Travel Guide, I trust your journey through its pages has sparked a flame of curiosity and wanderlust. Antalya, a gem nestled on the Turkish Riviera, is not just a destination; it's a tapestry of experiences waiting to be unraveled.

Antalya's allure extends beyond its historical charm; it embraces the breathtaking beauty of nature. From the majestic Düden Waterfalls cascading into the Mediterranean to the ancient wonders of Perge and Aspendos, every corner tells a story of a landscape shaped by time. The Taurus Mountains stand as silent sentinels, guarding the secrets of the region and providing a backdrop to adventures waiting to be explored.

The culinary journey in Antalya is not just a feast for the taste buds, but a cultural odyssey. From the tantalizing flavors of local markets to the sophistication of fine dining, every meal is an invitation to savor the essence of Turkish cuisine. As the sun sets over Kaleiçi, the ancient city center, the city comes alive with the echoes of history, vibrant street life, and the melody of folk music and dance.

For those seeking outdoor thrills, Antalya unveils a playground of possibilities. Whether you're trekking through the rugged landscapes of the Taurus Mountains, diving into the azure depths of the

Mediterranean, or simply basking in the sun on Konyaaltı Beach, the region caters to every adventurer's spirit. Yet, amidst the excitement, there are pockets of serenity—boutique stays in Kaleiçi and coastal resorts offering a tranquil escape.

The proposed weeklong itinerary is a mere glimpse into the myriad experiences Antalya has to offer. From the sunrise spectacle at Fitz Roy to the enchanting ruins of Perge, each day is crafted to provide a holistic experience. Yet, Antalya invites you to wander beyond the suggested path, to discover your own hidden gems, and to create memories that are uniquely yours.

As you venture into the enchanting realm of Antalya, may each moment be a chapter in your personal travelog. Whether you find solace in the whispers of ancient ruins or thrill in the adrenaline of outdoor pursuits, Antalya welcomes you with open arms, inviting you to become part of its ever-evolving story. Safe travels, and may your journey through Antalya be as boundless as the horizon over the Mediterranean.

Printed in Great Britain
by Amazon

42621569R00069